This book Belongs to

_____

Lapdogs, Love and Lattes

A Relaxing Color Therapy Book

Coloring is not just for kids. It has been proven to be an excellent way for adults to destress, create mindfulness and slow down from daily life, all while enjoying an activity that you can truly make your own. Every effort has been made to ensure that this is an enjoyable way to spend your time, but paper quality is something we don't have control over with this method of publishing, so please use the included sheet of paper behind your artwork to ensure that your chosen pens or markers do not bleed through to the next page. All pages are single sided to allow for framing and to help protect the next artwork.

There is no right or wrong way to color in the images in this book, and you are free to choose the tools you wish to work with. Markers, paint, colored pencils, pens – the choices are unlimited.

Sit back and unwind and let your stress melt away while you spread color across the pages.

Relax and enjoy this calming activity.

Color Test Page

Test your colors here

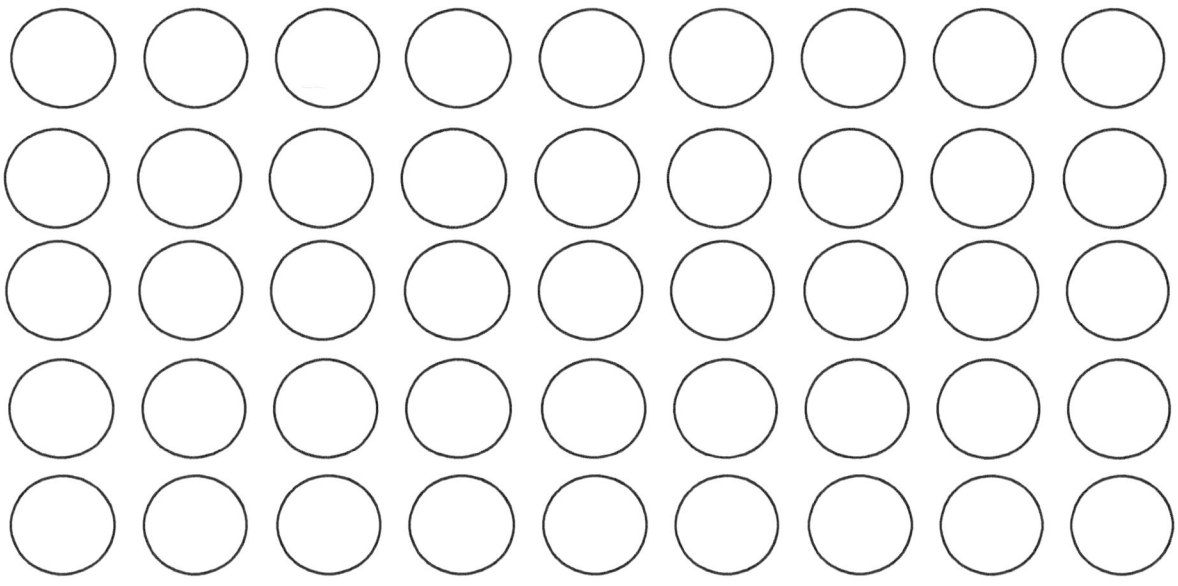

Cut out this page and insert behind the page you are currently coloring.

9

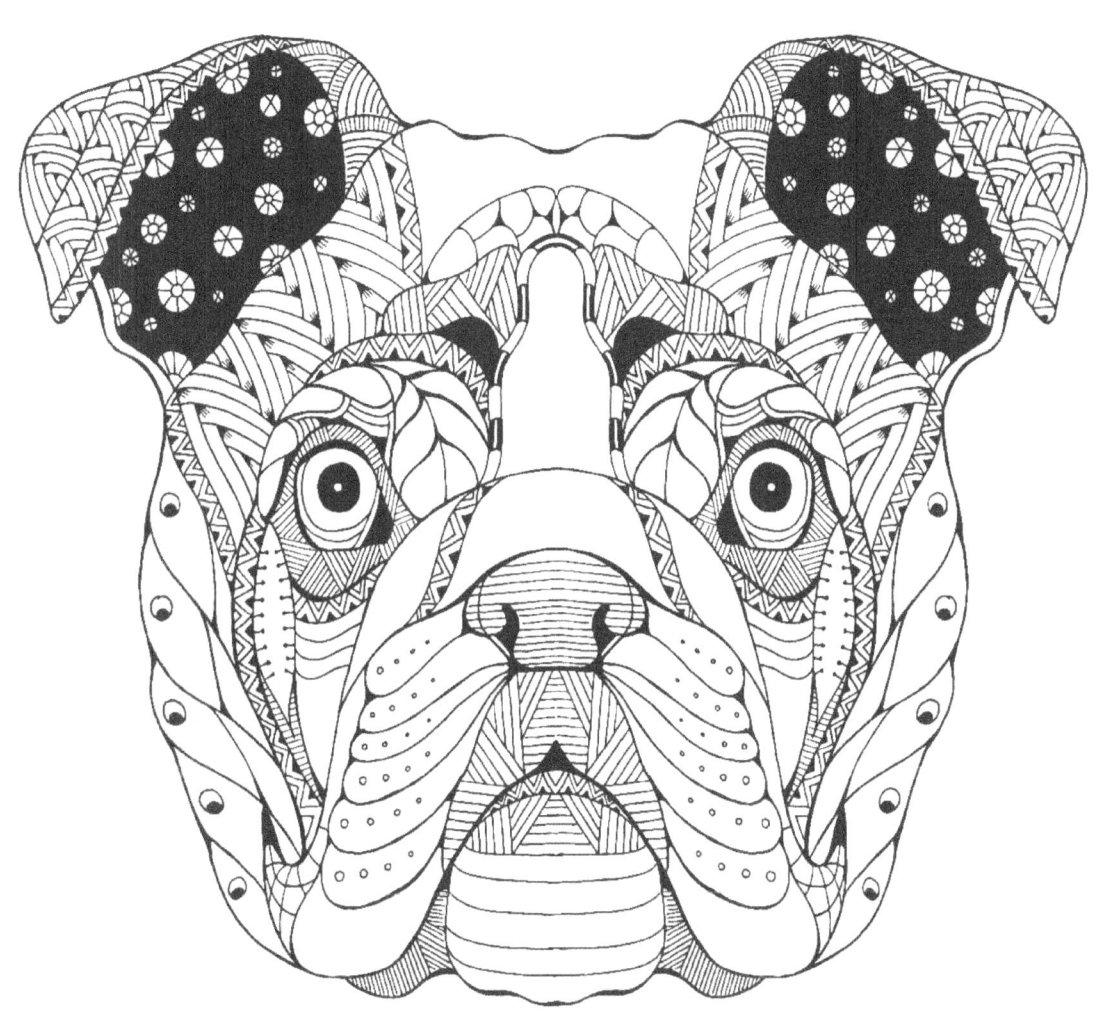

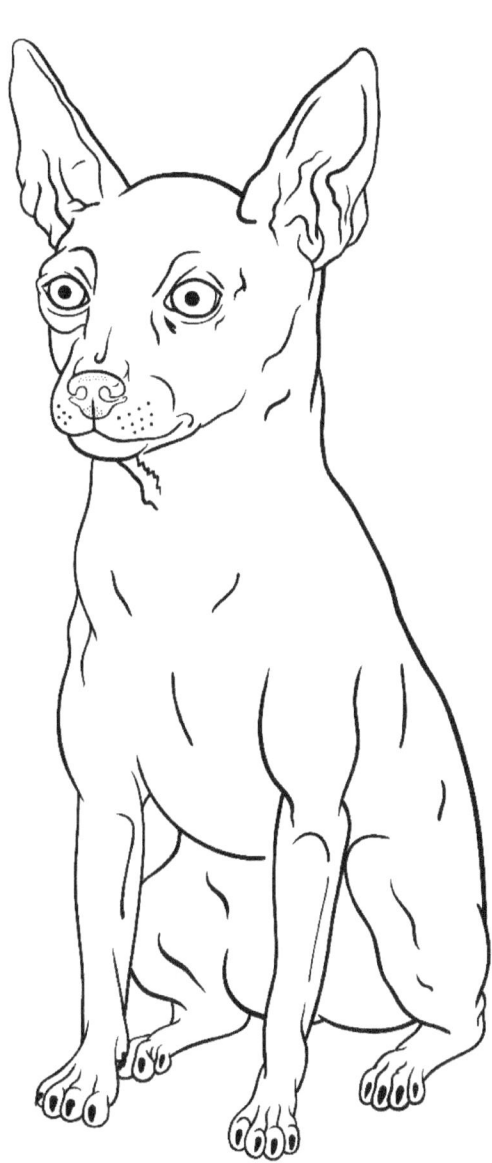

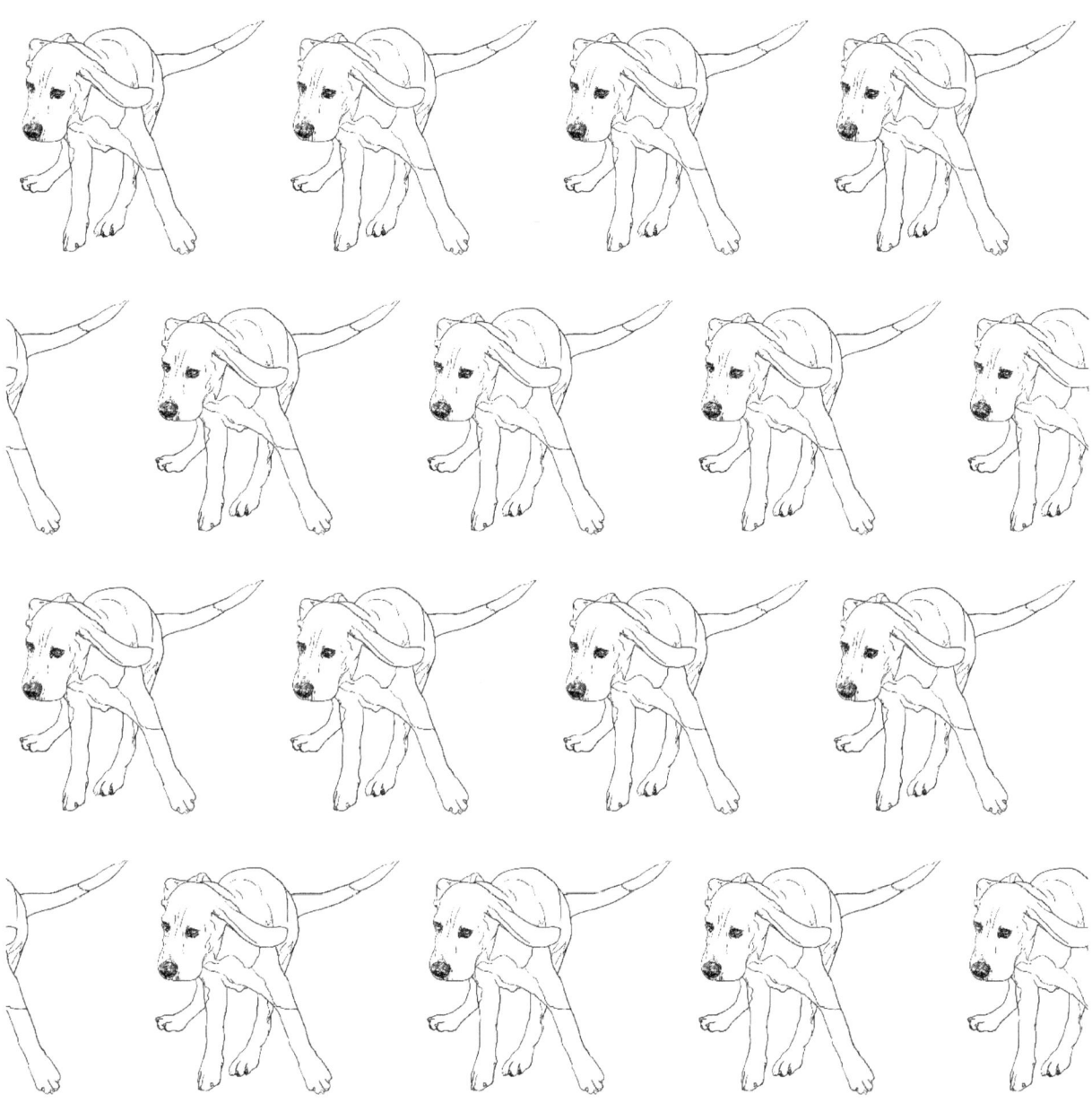

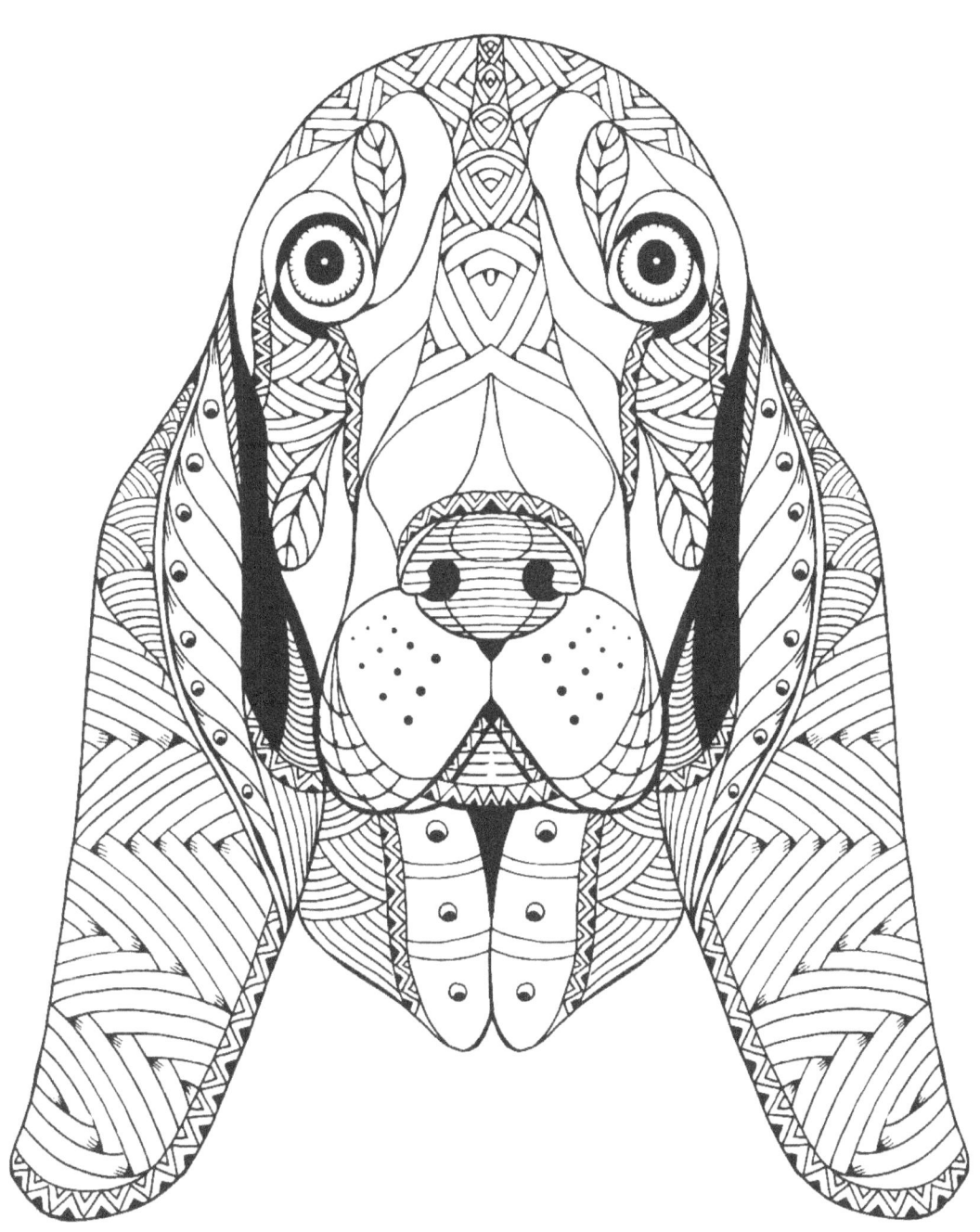